14. 20

# The United States

# North Dakota

Anne Welsbacher
**ABDO & Daughters**

# visit us at
# www.abdopub.com

Published by Abdo & Daughters, 4940 Viking Drive, Suite 622, Edina, Minnesota 55435.
Copyright © 1998 by Abdo Consulting Group, Inc., Pentagon Tower, P.O. Box 36036,
Minneapolis, Minnesota 55435 USA. International copyrights reserved in all countries.
No part of this book may be reproduced in any form without written permission from the
publisher.

Printed in the United States.

Cover and Interior Photo credits: Peter Arnold, Inc., SuperStock, Archive Photos

Edited by Lori Kinstad Pupeza
Contributing editor Brooke Henderson
Special thanks to our Checkerboard Kids—John Hansen, Stephanie McKenna, Raymond
Sherman, Grace Hansen

All statistics taken from the 1990 census; The Rand McNally Discovery Atlas of The
United States.

## Library of Congress Cataloging-in-Publication Data

Welsbacher, Anne, 1955-
    North Dakota / Anne Welsbacher.
    p.  cm. -- (The United States.)
    Includes index.
    Summary: Examines the geography, history, natural resources, people, and
    sports of the Flickertail State.
    ISBN 1-56239-896-2
    1. North Dakota--Juvenile literature. [1. North Dakota.] I. Title. II. Series:
    United States (Series)
    F636.3.W44  1998
    978.4--dc21                     97-31415
                                     CIP
                                     AC

# Contents

# Welcome to North Dakota

North Dakota is named for the Dakotas, some of the Native American people who lived in the area long ago. Today, many Native Americans still live in North Dakota. And two times every year, people from all over the country come to North Dakota to celebrate their **heritage**.

North Dakota has rich land with many farms. More sunflower seeds grow in North Dakota than in any other state! North Dakota also has lots of wildlife parks for visitors to enjoy.

North Dakota has many flickertail ground squirrels. For this reason it is called the Flickertail State. It also is called the Peace Garden State. This is because the International Peace Garden lies in both North Dakota and its neighbor to the north, Canada.

*The Badlands, North Dakota.*

# Fast Facts

## NORTH DAKOTA

**Capital**
Bismarck (49,256 people)
**Area**
69,299 square miles
(179,484 sq km)
**Population**
641,364 people
Rank: 47th
**Statehood**
November 2, 1889
(39th state admitted)
**Principal rivers**
Missouri River
Red River
**Highest point**
White Butte;
3,506 feet (1,069 m)
**Largest city**
Fargo (74,111 people)
**Motto**
Liberty and union, now and
forever, one and inseparable
**Song**
"North Dakota Hymn"
**Famous People**
Louis L'Amour, Maxwell
Anderson, Peggy Lee, Eric
Severeid, Lawrence Welk

*S*tate Flag

*W*ild Prairie Rose

*W*estern
Meadowlark

*A*merican Elm

# About North Dakota

## The Peace Garden State

**Detail area**

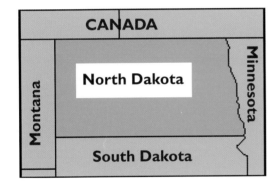

## ND

North Dakota's
abbreviation

**Borders:** west (Montana), north (Canada), east (Minnesota), south (South Dakota)

# Nature's Treasures

North Dakota has much rich soil.  It is good for farming. The Red River Valley, in North Dakota, has some of the best farmland in the world!

The Great Plains area has shale and limestone. West of the Red River Valley is sandy soil.

A very big oil field is in the western part of the state. This area also has lots of coal.  In the southwest there is clay in the land.  Some of this clay is used to make pottery.

*Opposite page:  Coal strip mining near North Dakota.*

# Beginnings

Native Americans arrived more than 10,000 years ago. They hunted big bison and other large animals. The first white people did not come to North Dakota until the 1700s. They came from Canada.

As the United States grew, people moved west. Many settlers moved all the way to California and other places.

Many Dakota and other Native Americans were pushed off of their lands. Sometimes they fought back in battles or surprise attacks. For this reason, many settlers were afraid of them, and did not begin to move into North Dakota until the late 1800s.

Many settlers were **immigrants**. They planted and grew so much wheat that their farms were called **bonanza** farms.

In 1889, North Dakota became the 39th state. Most settlers became farmers. Others built railroads, worked in mills to turn the wheat into flour, or set up banks.

In the 1900s, farmers battled **droughts** and other hardships.

In the 1940s, a big dam was built in North Dakota. It helped supply power and water for the farms. Later, oil was found in the state! Today, mining is another kind of work in North Dakota.

*A Native American encampment in North Dakota, 1800s.*

## B.C. to 1700s

### Old Times

 100 million years ago dinosaurs rule the land now called North Dakota.

 1000: Mandan, Hidatsa, and Arikara people grow corn, sunflowers, and beans.  They hunt buffalo and live in sod homes.

 1700s: French **explorers** begin to arrive.

# North Dakota

## B.C. to 1700s

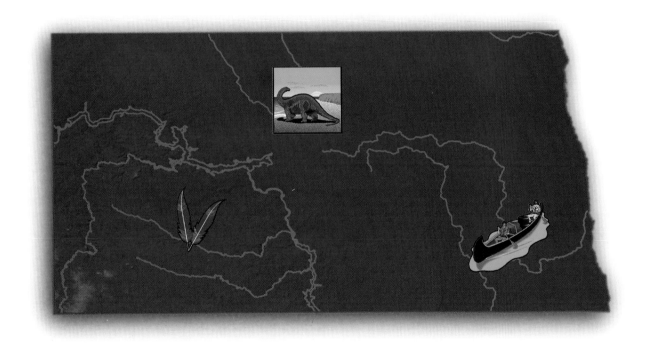

# 1861 to 1875

### Slow Growing

1861: The Dakota Territory is made. It includes the land that today is South Dakota and North Dakota.

1873: The first railroad is built in North Dakota. It now is easier to come to the state.

1875: **Bonanza** farms begin to grow big harvests of wheat.

# North Dakota

## 1861 to 1875

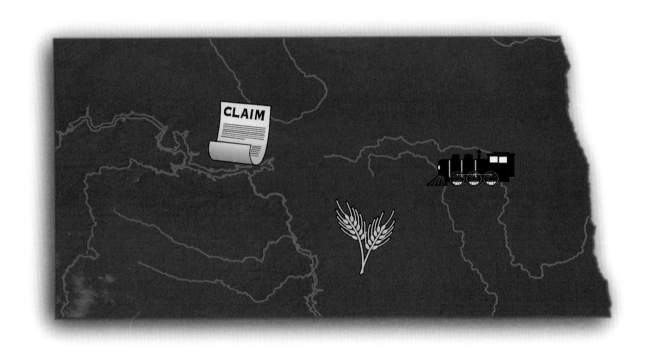

# 1800s to 1900s

### Statehood and Beyond

 Late 1800s: Cattle ranches begin in western North Dakota.

 1889: North Dakota becomes the 39th state.

 1930s: **Droughts** and dust storms hurt the land, water, and farms.

 1946-1960: The Garrison Dam is built.

 1997: Floods in eastern North Dakota, in the Red River Valley, destroy homes, property, and lives.

# North Dakota

## 1800s to 1900s

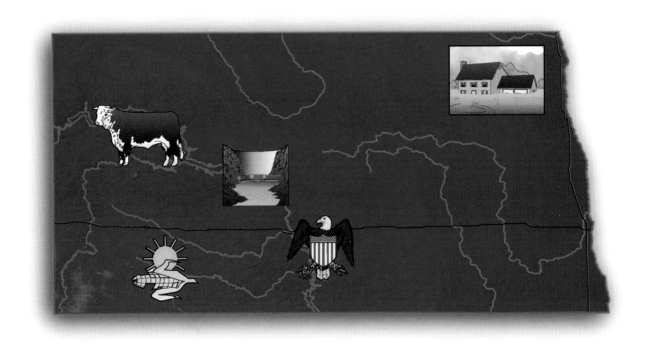

# North Dakota's People

Around 640,000 people live in North Dakota. That number might look big, but for most states, that number is very small.

The city of San Francisco has more people in it than the whole state of North Dakota! Only three states have fewer people in them than North Dakota.

About half the people live in cities. Most of these cities are small. Some people live on farms or on **reservations**.

Lawrence Welk was born in Strasburg, North Dakota. He was a famous band leader. His band played polka music in shows and on TV.

Singer Peggy Lee was born in Jamestown, North Dakota. She sang jazz music. She also was the voice of the poodle named Peg in the movie *Lady and the Tramp*.

Phyllis Frelich, from Devils Lake, helped start a theatre for the deaf and starred in a famous play about a deaf woman. The famous news reporter Eric Severeid was from North Dakota. Movie and TV actor Angie Dickinson also was born in North Dakota.

Roger Maris, also from North Dakota, holds the record for most home runs hit in one season while playing with the Yankees.

**Angie Dickinson**

**Lawrence Welk**

**Roger Maris**

# North Dakota's Cities

The largest city in North Dakota is Fargo. A lot of people in Fargo work in meat packing and build farm machines.

Bismarck, the second largest city, is the capital of North Dakota. It is on the Missouri River.

Grand Forks is the third largest city. It also is near a river, the Red River. Minot is the fourth largest city in North Dakota.

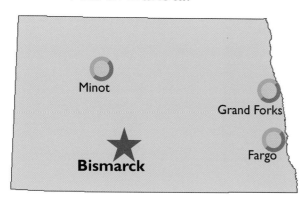

*Opposite page: The State Capitol in Bismarck, North Dakota.*

# North Dakota's Land

North Dakota is shaped like a sturdy box. Its bottom is a little wider than its top. The land is divided into three different regions.

Almost the entire western half of North Dakota is the Missouri Plateau region. This area is covered with steep hills and lowlands. The Missouri River cuts through the area, too, running across the state.

In the southwest corner of the Missouri Plateau are the **Badlands**. People from around the world visit this area. The Badlands are colorful clay, sand, and rock formations that were made from the effects of wind, frost, and rain.

Near the Badlands is the highest point in the state—White Butte.

Missouri plateau

Glacial Drift Prairie

Red River valley

In the far eastern part of the state is the Red River Valley region. A long time ago, this area was the bottom of a lake. Today, the soil is rich and the land is flat. It has some of the best farmland in the world! The region has been called the breadbasket of the world because the wheat is later turned into bread.

In between these regions is the third region—Glacier Drift Prairie. This area is filled with rolling hills, streams, and valleys. The Turtle Mountains and many lakes are in this area, too.

*A rock formation in the Badlands.*

# North Dakota at Play

North Dakota has more than 60 **wildlife sanctuaries**—more than any other state in the country!

The Theodore Roosevelt National Park is one of the best-loved of these parks. It is in the **Badlands** area. The park is named after a United States president who loved the North Dakota land. It has many pretty cliffs that rise high into the sky.

People also enjoy the Chase Lake National Wildlife Refuge. It is the largest **breeding ground** for pelicans in all of North America!

The United Tribes Powwow is held in Bismarck, North Dakota, every fall. People from all over the United States and Canada come to dance, sing, and eat foods like wild rice and corn soup.

Bonanzaville, USA, in West Fargo, shows what the towns were like in the 1800s. It has a church, sod houses, schoolhouse, log cabin, and jail.

Writing Rock Historic Site is near Grenora. It is a big rock with many pictures carved into it by Native Americans from a long time ago.

*A wildlife refuge in North Dakota.*

# North Dakota at Work

Many North Dakotans are farmers. They grow more wheat than in any other state except Kansas. They also grow sunflower seeds and flax. Flax is used to make rope and some kinds of cloth.

North Dakotans work on ranches, make farm machines, or put foods into packages. Others mine oil, coal, and gas from the land.

Many North Dakotans sell things like foods, cars, and tractors. Others are lawyers, doctors, or nurses. Many fix cars and trucks.

People also teach in **colleges** or on **reservations**. People work at all kinds of places in North Dakota.

A farmer at work in his field.

# Fun Facts

•North Dakota and South Dakota were one big area before they became states. Then they were cut into two and made into states at the same time. The President mixed up the papers so no one would ever know which was first to become a state. That way, neither state could say it was more important. Together they were the 39th and the 40th states. Today, we follow the alphabet. Since "N" comes before "S," we say that North Dakota is the 39th state and South Dakota is the 40th.

•Most of the lignite coal that is mined in the United States comes from the western part of North Dakota.

•A golf course in North Dakota lies partway in Canada. On some holes people playing this golf course can hit the ball all the way to another country!

•During the winter when there isn't much snow, North Dakotans say they have "snirt"—part snow and part dirt.

•The first woman who was a speaker for the State House of Representatives was North Dakota's Minnie Craig.
•Cream of Wheat cereal was first made in Grand Forks, North Dakota, in 1893.

*These kids are having fun playing in the snow.*

# Glossary

**Badlands:** a stretch of land in western North Dakota and South Dakota; the Dakota people called them "bad" lands because they were rocky and sometimes hard to travel through, but they are pretty to visit and look at.

**Bonanza:** something that brings great riches.

**Border:** the edge of something.

**Breeding ground:** a place where birds and animals come to have babies and take care of them.

**College:** a school you can go to after high school.

**Drought:** long period of time with no rain or snow.

**Explorer:** a person who looks for new lands and goes to unknown areas.

**Heritage:** something handed down from parents to children, for many years that helps say who they are; their traditions and customs; people celebrate their heritage at events like powwows.

**Immigrant:** a person who comes from another country.

**Reservation:** an area of land set aside for Native Americans to live on.

**Wildlife sanctuary:** a park where animals and plants can live safely, and people can come to see them.

# Internet Sites

**North Dakota "Mountain" Biking**
http://www2.stellarnet.com/~jwaltzer/ndmb/index.htm
The most "famous" mountain biking destination in North Dakota is the Badlands. The North Dakota Badlands have been featured in at least two popular mountain biking magazines. Some even go so far as to say that the Badlands are the next Moab. Without a doubt, there is some fine riding here.

**MEDORA: Historic Cowtown Amid Scenic Splendor**
http://www.glness.com/tourism/html/west/WestMedora.html
Medora gets its name from the beautiful wife of a wealthy French nobleman, the Marquis de Mores, who founded the town in 1883. For her, the Marquis built an elegant 28-room chateau, which was their home for two years. Now a State Historic Site, the Chateau de Mores has been exquisitely preserved, and is open daily during the vacation season. This site shows you the grand history of North Dakota.

These sites are subject to change. Go to your favorite search engine and type in North Dakota for more sites.

# PASS IT ON

## Tell Others Something Special About Your State

To educate readers around the country, pass on interesting tips, places to see, history, and little unknown facts about the state you live in. We want to hear from you!

**To get posted on ABDO & Daughters website, E-mail us at "mystate@abdopub.com"**

# Index